Let's Go to London!

Kaye Umansky
Illustrated by Adrienne Salgado

A & C Black • London

First published 2007 by
A & C Black Publishers Ltd
38 Soho Square, London, W1D 3HB

www.acblack.com

Text copyright © 2007 Kaye Umansky
Illustrations copyright © 2007 Adrienne Salgado

The rights of Kaye Umansky and Adrienne Salgado to be
identified as the author and illustrator of this work respectively
have been asserted by them in accordance with the
Copyrights, Designs and Patents Act 1988.

ISBN 978-0-7136-8539-8

A CIP catalogue for this book is available from the British Library.

This book is produced using paper that is made from wood grown
in managed, sustainable forests. It is natural, renewable and
recyclable. The logging and manufacturing processes conform
to the environmental regulations of the country of origin.

Printed and bound in Great Britain by MPG Books Limited.

Contents

Characters

The Actor – Aubrey Valentine
He has written a play.

The Doctor – Edmund Leech
Rather creepy.

The Farm girl – Meggie Wilkins
A simple country wench.

The Thief – Dot Doxy
A tough old tramp, who can't be trusted.

The Cook – Mrs Briggs
A motherly sort.

The Extra – Timothy Dogsbody
Willing, but sometimes not very able.

Glossary

Groundlings – the audience who stood in the yard. The nobles sat in the gallery.

Justice of the Peace – a law enforcer.

The Lord Chamberlain's Men – Shakespeare's company of actors.

Night-soil cart horse – night soil is human waste. Horse-pulled carts would come around at night to try and dispose of it.

Quarter Session – a court presided over by the Justice of the Peace.

Shank's pony – an expression meaning to walk.

Tiring room – a changing room where actors put on their costumes.

Walking mort – a woman tramp.

Prologue

A fanfare of trumpets. The cast enter and stand in line. **Aubrey** *steps forward. He is flamboyantly dressed. He snatches off his heavily plumed hat, and strikes a dramatic pose.*

Aubrey The trumpet sounds! Our play begins!
> Thrice welcome, everyone.
> 'Tis time to cast your cares away
> And have a bit of fun!
>
> Forget the plague! Forget the filth!
> (For these are Tudor times)
> And lose yourself in this, our tale,
> Which, you will notice, rhymes.

Meggie No, it doesn't.

Aubrey What?

Meggie It doesn't always rhyme. My bits don't.

Aubrey Ah. Well, that's because you only have a small, unimportant part. Naturally, being a professional actor, I've given all the clever rhyming stuff to myself.

Mrs Briggs So we've noticed.

Aubrey And why not? I am a member of the Lord Chamberlain's Men. I trained at the Globe, with Shakespeare. Most people have heard of me. Aubrey Valentine, actor. Quite frankly, I'm slumming it with you lot.

Mrs Briggs Why didn't you get proper actors, then?

Aubrey Couldn't afford 'em. Now, can we get on with the play, please?

Dot What do you know about slummin' it? I can tell you about slummin' it. I'm a tramp. I *live* in a slum.

Meggie I thought tramps lived in ditches.

Dot That's when we're in the country. In town, I got a proper slum.

Aubrey Oh, be quiet. And stop giving yourselves all these words to say, they're not in the script. (*To the audience.*) I'm sorry, ladies and gentlemen, this is what happens when you work with amateurs. Look, you've both got unimportant parts. That's because you're women. By rights, if we're going to be really authentic, you're not even *supposed* to be acting. These are Tudor times. It's customary for men to play the female roles.

Timothy Does that mean I might have to be a girl?

Aubrey If necessary, yes. You're the

extra, Timothy, you play all the parts called for by the script. We did discuss this, you know. (*Sighs and addresses the audience*.) I'm so sorry, ladies and gentlemen, this isn't supposed to be happening. I've written this rather wonderful play. It's called *Let's Go To London*! Once it's whipped into shape, I intend to show it to Shakespeare. It has an interesting cross section of characters, but sadly I can't afford to use professional actors, so I'm stuck with amateurs, who have agreed to perform it for your delectation.

Edmund And a fee.

Aubrey Yes. A small fee.

Dot Not that small. We're takin' time out from our real lives to do this.

Edmund Indeed. I am a busy man. Time is money.

Aubrey Yes, yes, we've been over this!

I've said you will be paid.

Mrs Briggs Just so long as that's clear.

Aubrey Shush. (*To the audience.*) To
continue. I shall be playing myself, of
course. Then I've assembled a doctor,
a cook, a farm girl and a tramp, who
will also play versions of themselves, in
character. That way, I don't have to train
them. Hopefully, all they have to do is
get the lines right.

Timothy What about me?

Aubrey Ah yes. And Timothy
Dogsbody, who will play anything he
is required.

Timothy But – girls? Aw, come on…

Aubrey Timothy. This is show biz. The
play's the thing. You say you want to be
an actor. Now's your chance to shine.

Timothy But – *girls*. What – in a dress
and that?

Aubrey If necessary, yes.

Mrs Briggs Well, he's not borrowing mine.

Meggie Or mine.

Dot Or mine.

Timothy Like I'd want to. (*Holds his nose.*)

Dot Less of your cheek. And excuse me, Master Valentine, goin' back to what you said, I ain't got an unimportant part. I got quite a bit to say for meself, I 'ave.

Edmund Only because you keep giving yourself extra lines. If you were able to follow the script, which you can't, because you're a foolish old woman who can't read, I think you'd find you have considerably fewer lines than me.

Dot What do you know about it?

Edmund Trust me, I'm a doctor.

I'm also a man. That makes me very, very clever and wise, unlike you uneducated females.

Dot Oooh. Get you!

Meggie It's not our fault nobody's taught us to read.

Aubrey (*annoyed*) Look, will you please keep to the script. The prologue's supposed to be short and to the point. I'd like to finish it before the groundlings start throwing fruit. Now, kindly step aside while I round things off in a proper manner. Ahem.

He strikes a dramatic pose.

>The time is ripe. Pin back your ears.
>The play begins at last.
>My name is Aubrey Valentine.
>I head our modest cast.

Dot No, you don't.

Aubrey Yes, I *do*.

Mrs Briggs Let him finish, Dot, or we'll be here all day.

Aubrey We take you to a riverbank
>All on a summer's day
>Where folk await the ferryman
>To take them on their way.

Their destination? London Town.
The home of Good Queen Bess.
But will they get there? Yes or no?
It's anybody's guess.

Edmund Is that it?

Aubrey Yes. We can now start Act One.
Take your places, please. Go on, go on!

Aubrey *shoos them offstage. They exit,
grumbling.*

Aubrey Ladies and gentlemen, lords
and ladies, uncouth yobs in the yard –
Let's Go To London!

Act One

Twittering birds. The riverbank. Enter
Meggie *with a wicker basket full of eggs.*
She peers offstage, looking for the ferryman
on the opposite bank. Enter **Edmund** *with*
his black doctor's bag.

Edmund Good day, young woman.
I take it you are waiting for the ferry?

Meggie (*curtseying*) I am, sir.

Edmund Your name?

Meggie Meggie Wilkins. Just a simple
farm girl, going to London to sell eggs
at St Bartholomew's Fayre. *Atchoo!*

Edmund Dear me. That's a nasty cold

16

you've got there. Too much yellow bile in the body. A session of blood-letting with leeches should do the trick.

Meggie Eh?

Edmund Trust me, I am a doctor. Edmund Leech is my name. Just a coincidence. I have the little fellows right here; it won't take a minute to apply them. (*Produces a bag full of squirming leeches from his bag.*)

Meggie Urggh! No, no, it's all right. It's just the pollen in the air.

Edmund Suit yourself. Of course, we could try cutting off your hair and smearing your head with fox grease and crushed beetle juice. If you're worried about shaving your head, I can do it for you. I'm a trained barber as well as a surgeon. (*Produces a large knife from his bag.*)

Meggie No, really, I'll be fine.

Enter **Dot**, *swathed in rags and carrying a long pole with a hook on the end.* **Meggie** *and* **Edmund** *hold their noses. She whiffs a bit. But then, so does everyone. These are Tudor times.*

Dot Is this the queue for the ferry?

Meggie Yes.

Edmund Kindly get to the back, foul old woman. Preferably downwind.

Dot Less of the foul old woman. Me name's Dot Doxy. *Mrs* Doxy to you. 'Ere! What you doin' with that big knife? Are you out to murder us?

Edmund Certainly not. I am a doctor.

Dot I knew it! You *are* out to murder us!

Edmund Nonsense. Begone, smelly old woman with your foul insinuations.

Dot Well, it's true. Everyone knows you lot kill more than you cure.

Edmund Well, if it comes to it, what are you doing with that hook on a pole?

Dot (*flustered*) What hook on a pole?

Edmund (*pointing*) *That* hook on a pole.

Dot Oh, right. *This* hook on a pole. I... um... I uses it to keep bears at bay.

Edmund A likely tale. You use it to hook clothes off washing lines and sell them down the market. I know your sort.

Dot Ah, shut yer trap. When's this ferry comin', I ain't got all day.

Everyone looks offstage.

Meggie I can see the ferryman on the opposite bank. He's got a tankard of ale, look. He's drooling. Oops! He's fallen over.

Dot Typical. Drunk, as usual. Anyone given 'im a shout? No? I will, then. OI! COME OVER 'ERE, YER LAZY BAG O'

GUTS, THERE'S PEOPLE WAITIN'!

Enter **Aubrey**. *He takes off his cap and gives a low, theatrical bow.*

Aubrey What ho, good folk, what uncouth caterwauling is this?

Edmund This foul old walking mort is shouting for the ferryman.

Dot Who you callin' a walkin' mort, saw bones? Blimmin' cheek.

Aubrey Saw bones? You are a doctor, sir?

Edmund I am, sir. Trust me.

Dot I wouldn't.

Meggie He wanted to shave my head and rub in fox grease just because I sneezed.

Aubrey Fox grease? Hmm, interesting. My sainted mother always swore by eating live spiders in butter. I'm not sure which was worse, sneezing or having a tickle in the throat.

All laugh, merrily.

Dot Spiders is for curing asthma, I always thought.

Edmund Oh dear me, no. How little you know, you ignorant old woman.

Swallowing frogs is the accepted cure for asthma. Us medical men know these things.

Dot I thought frogs was warts.

Edmund That's *toads*. You swallow frogs for asthma and rub on toads for warts. First thing you learn in medical school. We used to chant it. Frog-for-asthma, toad-for-warts, frog-for-asthma, toad-for-warts. Like that.

Dot If you're so clever, what are you doin' hangin' around 'ere?

Edmund I have been touring the countryside collecting plants, herbs, bats, worms and leeches, if it's any of your business. On my return to London, I will make them into essential oils. I then plan to publish a definitive guide to medicine, with a special chapter devoted to bleeding.

Aubrey Indeed? Well, good luck to you,

sir. I too am returning to London, to rejoin the Lord Chamberlain's Men at Shakespeare's famous Globe Theatre. As you may have guessed from my clear speaking voice, flamboyant dress and good hat, I am an actor!

He bows to the audience and hopes for applause.

Meggie Oooh! Really?

Aubrey Yes. Aubrey Valentine's the name. Do you want my autograph?

Meggie No point, sir, I can't read. I've never been to the theatre.

Aubrey No? You should. It only costs a penny to stand in the yard with the groundlings. Three pennies will buy you a balcony seat with a cushion. But looking at your bare feet and humble dress, I doubt a poor wench like you can afford that.

Meggie I can't afford the time, either. I've got to sell my eggs then get straight back to the farm, Mother said.

Timothy (*offstage*) Excuse me? Master Valentine?

Aubrey What?

Timothy When are we getting to my bit?

Aubrey Soon. Shush. We're waiting for the last character to arrive.

Timothy Well, hurry up. I'm getting fed up back here. The bear's making horrible noises.

Dot What bear?

Aubrey The bear that chases us off at the end of Act Three.

Meggie What – a *real* one?

Aubrey Certainly. This is Tudor theatre. We don't do things by halves. Don't worry, he's toothless. (*Shouts.*) Give him a piece of cheese, he likes that.

Enter **Mrs Briggs** *with a basket containing a rabbit pie.*

Mrs Briggs Did I hear something about a bear?

Aubrey Look, can we please stop mentioning the bear. It'll spoil the element of surprise.

Mrs Briggs Nobody said nothing about a real bear. I've got a rabbit pie in my basket. Supposing he smells it? I want danger money.

Aubrey We'll discuss that later, Mrs Briggs. Your line, I think, doctor.

Edmund Right. Ahem. Good morrow to you, mistress. Do you await the ferry?

Mrs Briggs Indeed I do, sir. The name's Mrs Briggs. I've just got a job as head housekeeper at one of the fine houses in

London Town. My brother got me the post. He's top footman. Got a uniform and everything.

Aubrey Well now, here's a merry coincidence. It appears that all of us are London bound. Each for a separate purpose, but all travelling the same road. Hail, fellows, well met, eh? Shall we go together?

Mrs Briggs We ain't going nowhere at this rate. Where's that ferryman?

Dot Over on the far bank, sleepin' it off. OI! WAKE UP, YOU TUB O' LARD!

Meggie I think he moved then. Try again, Dot.

Dot HEY! YOU! SQUIFF HEAD!

Timothy (*offstage*) Wha?

Dot YOU'RE THE FERRYMAN, AINCHA?

Timothy (*sounding drunken*) Yesh. That I be. Sho?

Dot SO GET YER FLIPPIN' FERRY OVER 'ERE! THERE'S FOLKS WAITIN', YOU SORRY SACK!

Timothy Lemme be. I'm on a break. Hic!

Dot I'LL GIVE YOU A BREAK! I'LL BREAK YER NECK IF YOU DON'T GET OVER 'ERE NOW!

Edmund I don't think using foul language and threats is the way to get prompt service, old woman. You've said quite enough.

Aubrey Quite right. This is a job for a man. EXCUSE ME, OVER THERE...

Edmund *elbows him to one side.*

Edmund Allow me. I have an excellent riverside manner.

Aubrey I think you'll find that the script calls for *me* to summon the ferryman.

Edmund Well, it shouldn't. As a doctor, I am clearly the man for the job. Ahem. Ahoy there, my man! Stir yourself immediately! We require ferrying forthwith! Look sharp! That is an order!

Mrs Briggs What's he doing?

Meggie He's sitting up.

Dot Now he's lying down again.

Meggie He's reaching for his tankard. He's up again.

Meggie Oh!

Mrs Briggs He made a rude sign. Well I never!

Dot (*snidely, to* **Edmund**) So much for doin' what the doctor ordered.

Edmund I don't believe it! The oaf is lying down again.

Mrs Briggs Public transport. It don't get any better.

Meggie Oh dear. This isn't getting us anywhere. What shall we do?

Aubrey There's a bridge a mile or two upriver. I suggest we cut our losses and walk.

Mrs Briggs (*sighs*) Shank's pony it is, then. Though I could do without this. Me corns are killing me.

Aubrey There's a tavern by the bridge. If we stride out, we'll make it by noon. I'll treat you all to a refreshing drink.

Dot Oooh! Ta.

Aubrey Come, companions all! Follow me!

Led by **Aubrey,** *they exit, stage right.*
Enter **Timothy,** *stage left, waving around*
a tankard. He addresses the audience.

Timothy That surprised you, didn't it?
You didn't expect to see the drunken
ferryman. Not much of a part, so I just
thought I'd nip on and show you my
costume. Not that it's particularly
interesting. Just a sort of brown tunic
thing. I wear the same in the next act,
with the addition of an apron, because
I'm playing the grumpy landlord...

Aubrey (*offstage*) Timothy! Get off!

Timothy Hear that? That's how I'm
treated, just because I'm the extra. Still,
I must remember the old saying. Big
trees from little acorns grow. Today
offstage ferryman; next week, Piglet.

Aubrey (*offstage*) Hamlet!

Timothy Oh yeah, Hamlet.

Aubrey (*offstage*) Off! Now!

Timothy Right, I'd better go. See you in the pub – *ow*!

Dot's *pole with a hook on the end fishes him off from the side.*

Act Two

A filthy, squalid drinking house. Three small barrels of mead are lined up against the wall. It is empty, apart from the **landlord,** *played by* **Timothy,** *who is wiping the table with a filthy rag. He pauses, blows his nose on the rag, then carries on wiping. Enter* **Aubrey, Edmund, Meggie, Mrs Briggs** *and* **Dot.**

Aubrey Here we are, the Bridgeside Tavern. Bit of a dump, but any port in a storm, as Sir Francis Drake would say.

Meggie Him being the well-known Tudor sailor.

Aubrey Correct. Not to be confused

with Sir Walter Raleigh, the other well-known Tudor sailor.

Mrs Briggs What 'ave Tudor sailors got to do with anything?

Aubrey Nothing. I put them in for educational purposes. Theatre can teach as well as entertain. Carry on, doctor.

Edmund So. This is a typical tavern, is it? It's a poor place, not what I'm used to at all, being a member of a private, highly exclusive gentlemen's drinking club. In my professional opinion, I think we are taking our lives in our hands, setting foot in here.

Mrs Briggs I don't care as long as I can take the weight off me feet!

Collapses onto the bench.

Aubrey That's it, you take it easy, Mrs Briggs. Mead all round, is it? Ho there, landlord! Five tankards of your best mead! Let no one say us actors don't know how to throw a merry party!

The **landlord** *points at* **Dot**.

Timothy I'm not serving her. Didn't you see the sign outside? No walking morts.

Dot Who are you calling a walking mort?

Timothy You. This is a decent house. You're bad luck. Besides, you whiff worse than a night-soil cart 'orse. You'll put the other customers off.

Meggie You don't have any other customers.

Timothy (*defiantly*) I do sometimes.

Meggie Who?

Timothy Two old men and a smelly dog.

Mrs Briggs Oh my! How do you cope?

Timothy Look, it's my tavern, my rules, an' I don't serve tramps. You'll have to wait outside. And you can take all the baggage with you an' all. I've had trouble in the past with people sneakin' off with bags full o' free pork scratchin's.

Mrs Briggs There ain't any free pork scratchin's.

Timothy That's 'cos they've been nicked. All bags outside. (*Points to* **Dot**.) Especially her.

Edmund I hope you're not referring to *my* bag. A doctor is never parted from his doctor's bag. I'll have you know there's a valuable leech collection in there.

Timothy All bags out, I said. They clutters the place up. If you don't like it, you can always go to the next tavern.

Aubrey (*walking to the door*) I think we might just do that, on principle, seeing as you are refusing to serve our friend here. Don't you worry, Mrs Doxy, you have our full support. (*To the* **landlord**.) How far is the next tavern?

Timothy Twenty-seven miles.

Aubrey (*he stops*) Oh.

Dot Ah, who cares, don't mind me. I'm used to it. I'll go outside and wait for you. Give us yer stuff. I'll keep an eye on it. I don't trust the folks hereabouts. They looks shifty.

Glaring at the **landlord,** *she collects the two baskets and* **Edmund***'s bag and turns to go.*

Aubrey Well, I think it's ridiculous. Quite frankly, landlord, I don't like your attitude.

Timothy An' I don't like your hat. That goes out an' all.

Aubrey You don't like my *hat?* What's wrong with it?

Timothy I don't like the colour.

Aubrey Well, I don't like this flyblown shack you call a tavern. I've a good mind to challenge you to a duel! Except I appear to have mislaid my sword.

Meggie You haven't got a sword?

Aubrey The costume budget wouldn't run to it.

Dot Give us yer hat, Master Valentine. It'll save time. I'll take good care of it.

Aubrey Oh – very well, if I must! But for two pins, I'd drub the rascal!

Crossly, he gives his hat to **Dot,** *who gives it a reverent brush.*

Dot Don't none of you worry about nuthin'. You all have a nice drink, take your time, I'll be right outside. Keepin' an eye on yer stuff.

Dot *winks at the audience. She clearly has treachery in mind. Exit, to audience boos.*

Meggie Poor old Dot.

Mrs Briggs Shame. We should have stood by her.

Edmund We should, we should.

Aubrey So. Mead all round then, is it?

All (*hastily*) Yes, please.

The **landlord** *busies himself with barrels and tankards. The others talk about him in an undertone.*

Edmund Extraordinary behaviour. It's not as though he's got standards to keep up. Look at the place – it's a pigsty. Not at all what us doctors are used to.

Meggie I don't think he trusts strangers.

Mrs Briggs Don't suppose he gets many round here.

Aubrey (*to* **Edmund**) These country types. They're so suspicious. Suspicious and superstitious and – and lots of other words ending in *ishus*. Um... I need to work on that line. Carry on, doctor.

Edmund I doubt whether they see a new face from one year to the other. They live such insulated lives, cut off from culture and learning and fashion and all the things one takes for granted in London Town.

Meggie Well, you do. Some of us ain't so lucky. I've never even been there. Have you, Mrs Briggs?

Mrs Briggs Just the once, for the job interview. Got trampled by a runaway horse and had me purse nicked. Takes a bit o' getting used to.

The **landlord** *plonks down their tankards. During the following conversation,* **Dot***'s pole with the hook on the end appears from the wings, secures a barrel of mead and slowly drags it off.*

Timothy That'll be four pence.

Aubrey We were just saying, you live a quiet life here, I gather.

Timothy Oh aye. An' that's the way I likes it.

Mrs Briggs Never been to London, then?

Timothy No. Why would I? Dirty. Noisy. Full o' thievin', murdererin' scum.

Edmund You're right there. Don't get me going on crime. I see it every day, through the windows of my exclusive club.

Timothy I wouldn't mind seein' 'er Majesty, mind. But I reckon she stays in 'er palace most o' the time. Keepin' out o' the way o' the cut throats an' murderers.

Meggie I'd love to see the queen. I bet she has fancy clothes and beautiful jewels and things. If I was her, I'd wear my crown in bed.

Mrs Briggs My brother saw her once, on a barge on the River Thames. It were painted red, white an' blue.

Meggie What was she doing?

Mrs Briggs Just bargin' around.

Aubrey A toast. To Good Queen Bess!

They stand and clink glasses.

All To Good Queen Bess!

They drink. **Meggie** *goes to exit.*

Mrs Briggs Ah. That hit the spot. Where are you going, Meggie?

Meggie Just popping out to see if Dot's all right. I'm feeling guilty, sitting here having a good time when she's all on her own.

Exit **Meggie**.

Timothy (*slowly and carefully*) One... two...

Aubrey What are you doing, landlord?

Timothy Countin' the barrels. I could have sworn there were three, but I only make it two. I'll try again. One... two....

Enter **Meggie**, *panic-stricken*.

Meggie Oh, my law! Oh! Oh!

Edmund Whatever is the matter, girl?

Meggie Dot's gone! An' taken all our stuff with her!

Aubrey What – my *hat*?

Mrs Briggs My pie?

Edmund Not my medical bag, surely?

Meggie All of it! And my eggs!

Timothy 'Ere! She's taken a barrel o' mead. I knew I was right!

Mrs Briggs Oooh! The schemin' old scallywag!

Aubrey She can't have gone far. Quick, let's catch her up!

All exit.

Act Three

Many hours later. A moonlit forest. Owls hoot. Enter **Dot**, *laden down with two baskets, the doctor's bag, and Aubrey's hat, which she wears on her head. She is kicking the barrel of mead before her, as if dribbling a football. She addresses the audience direct.*

Dot Phew! I gotta sit down, I'm puffed.

She collapses onto a handy tree stump.

I suppose you want to boo me. Go on, then, see if I care. (*Pauses for boos.*) Got it out of your systems? Good. Now you can shut up and leave me be. I been hobblin' along for hours, up hill an' down. I think I've thrown 'em off. I deserves a rest.

They'll never find me in this forest. Now, where's that rabbit pie?

She rummages in Mrs Brigg's basket, breaks off a huge piece of pie and chews it.

I don't know why you're lookin' at me like that. You ought to feel sorry for me. Poor old woman, always on the road. No money, no possessions, except me trusty hook on a pole. Think it pays well, hookin' clothes off washin' lines? 'Course it don't. You can't blame me if I makes the most of a golden opportunity.

She pauses and looks guilty.

Yeah, all right. So I feels a bit bad. But only a bit. I got a pie, a medical bag, a dozen eggs, a barrel o' grog and a fancy hat, so I can put up with that. I'll just finish off the mead. (*Swigs from the barrel.*) Lovely. (*Shakes the barrel.*) Shame it's all gone. I wonder if these eggs is cooked?

She takes one out, breaks it and tosses the shell over her shoulder.

Nope. I'll fry 'em up later, when the pie's gone down. Now then. What's in this bag, I wonder?

She picks up Edmund's bag and fiddles with the clasp. After a fight, she gets it open and peers in.

Oh my! A hacksaw, blades, scalpels, toadstools, poison ivy, stingin' nettles – glad I'm not his patient. What's this bag o' wiggly things? (*Examines the bag of leeches.*) Lunch? (*Peers into the bag.*) Oo-er. Some of 'em 'ave got out and are wiggling round. Brrrr. Get back in, you little devils.

Offstage shouts and crashings.

Aubrey She went this way! Follow me, everyone!

Meggie Which way? I can't see you!

Mrs Briggs Where is everybody?

Edmund Through the trees! Through the trees!

Dot Oh my! I'd better skeddadle!

*She hastily gathers up her stolen goods and exits, kicking the barrel. Enter **Aubrey**, alone, at a run.*

Aubrey Come along, everyone, follow me. Oh. Everyone? Where are you? That's funny, I thought they were behind me.

*He peers around. Enter **Edmund**, backwards. Slowly, they back towards each other. They collide, hilariously. They both jump and spin round.*

Aubrey Oh! Doctor! There you are! Where are the others?

Edmund Speaking as a doctor, we seem to have lost them.

Aubrey I told them we should stay close

together. It's easy to get lost in the forest. (*Shouts*.) Hallooooo? Hallooooo? Anyone there? Meggie? Mrs Briggs? Where are you?

Silence. Then a menacing, offstage growl.

Timothy Grrrrrrrrrrr!

Aubrey What was that?

Edmund Speaking as a medical man, I would say it was a bear.

Aubrey Oh no!

Timothy (*closer this time*) Grrrrrrrrrrr!

Edmund This is bad. What to do, I wonder? We could try bleeding it, but I don't have my leeches.

Aubrey I could fight it. Ah, if I only had a sword! A sword, a sword, my kingdom for a sword!

Edmund You still don't have a sword?

Aubrey No. So it's onto Plan C.

Edmund Which is?

Aubrey RUN!

They exit, at speed, shouting, 'Help, help, a bear!' Enter **Timothy**, *growling, in a furry rug.*

Timothy Grrrrrrrrr! (*To the audience.*) Yep. It's me. You weren't expecting a real bear, were you? This is an amateur production, remember? We can't afford the true thing. All that stuff earlier about there being a real bear was just acting. If we can't even afford a sword, what makes you think we...

Enter **Aubrey**.

Aubrey (*crossly*) What are you playing at, Timothy?

Timothy I'm just saying there isn't a real bear.

Aubrey Well, don't. It's ruining the play. Theatre's all about illusion. You're supposed to stay hidden and growl, not come rushing on in a stupid, furry rug.

Timothy Sorry.

Aubrey Just stick to the script, all right?

Timothy All right. What do we do now?

Aubrey I suppose you'll have to chase me off again.

Timothy Right. Ready?

Aubrey Yes, yes, go on.

Timothy Grrrrrrrrr!

Aubrey Aargh! Help! A bear! A bear!

Exit **Aubrey,** *pursued by the bear. Enter* **Meggie,** *helping* **Mrs Briggs,** *who is hobbling.*

Meggie Come on, Mrs Briggs, you can do it.

Mrs Briggs Ooh, me feet. I got to sit down. (*She collapses on the tree stump.*)

Meggie That's it, you have a little rest.

Mrs Briggs Ooh! Meggie! Look! I've just noticed!

Meggie What?

Mrs Briggs There's pie crumbs all around this stump. And, look, there's a feather off Master Valentine's hat! And – aargh! A runaway leech! (*Jumps up and brushes her skirt.*) I don't want leeches in me breeches.

Meggie Look! There are barrel tracks in the mud! And here's a broken eggshell!

Mrs Briggs You know what this means, don't you?

Meggie What?

Mrs Briggs All them clues point to one thing. (*Dramatically.*) Dot was 'ere! We gotta tell the others!

Meggie You wait here and take it easy, and I'll find them. Yoohoo! Master Valentine? Doctor? Where are you?

Exit **Meggie***, leaving* **Mrs Briggs** *alone. She sits on the tree stump and addresses the audience direct.*

53

Mrs Briggs Fancy that cunning, old tyke making off with my rabbit pie. I was looking forward to that. There's nothing like home cooking. O' course, I'll have a team to help me when I take over the kitchens at the Big House in London. They does a lot of entertainin'. I'll be in charge of the menus and the orderin' and I get to boss the skivvies…

She breaks off. A low growl comes from offstage.

Timothy Grrrrrrrrr!

Mrs Briggs (*jumping up*) Oh, my heart! Whatever was that?

Enter **Timothy**, *as the* **landlord**, *at a run.*

Timothy (*furiously*) Where is she? Where's the walking mort?

Mrs Briggs Well, she *was* here, but she's moved on now.

Timothy You just wait till I catch up

with her! I'll make her swallow her own pole, hook-end first.

Mrs Briggs Shush. Stop shouting. I thought I heard a growling noise.

Timothy You did?

Mrs Briggs Yep. It came from that way. (*Points offstage.*)

Timothy What sort of growling noise?

Mrs Briggs Like a bear.

Timothy A bear?

Mrs Briggs A bear. Shush. Listen. It might come again.

Pointlessly, they wait.

Timothy I don't think it will, you know.

Mrs Briggs Shush! Listen!

They wait some more.

55

Timothy (*calling*) Um – Master Valentine?

Aubrey (*offstage*) What?

Timothy Something's gone a bit wrong. Come here a minute.

Enter **Aubrey**.

Aubrey What now?

Timothy Got a problem. We're waiting for the bear to growl.

Aubrey Yes? And?

Timothy Well, he can't, because I'm playing him. And right now, I'm on stage playing the landlord.

Aubrey Oh. Yes, I see what you mean. Merely a temporary hiccup, we can get round it.

Mrs Briggs How?

Aubrey Us professionals are trained to

cope when things go a little awry. Watch and learn. This is called improvisation. (*Shouts.*) Doctor! Meggie! Hallooo there!

Enter **Edmund**, *together with* **Meggie.**

Aubrey Ah, there you are, doctor. I've been looking for you everywhere. We must've got separated when we were running away from the bear.

Meggie What bear?

Aubrey The one that chased us earlier. (*Pointedly, to* **Timothy**.) The bear that went that way. (**Timothy** *looks blank.*) That way. (**Timothy** *still fails to take the hint.*) If you get my meaning.

Edmund Mrs Briggs, Meggie was saying you spotted a stray leech belonging to me. Did you see which way it went? Here, my little one, come to Daddy…

He searches for the leech.

Meggie There's other clues as well, Master Valentine. See the broken eggshell? All them clues point to one thing. (*Dramatically*.) Dot was here!

Mrs Briggs Excuse me, that's my line.

Meggie I know. Sorry.

Aubrey *spots the feather from his hat and swoops on it with a happy cry.*

Aubrey 'Zounds! Meggie, you're right! Here's a feather from my hat!

Mrs Briggs Don't forget to mention my pie crumbs. They're a good clue.

Aubrey And, look! The tracks made by the barrel. (*Pointedly, to* **Timothy**.) Landlord, why don't you run on ahead and see where they lead?

Timothy Why? What are you going to do?

Aubrey We will rest here a while, then

follow in your trail. Which is probably in the same direction *as the bear went.*

Timothy I don't see why I should 'ave to – oh, *I* get it. You've got to get me offstage, right? So that I can be the bear?

Aubrey (*through gritted teeth*) Yes.

Timothy Right. (*Shouts.*) Where are you, you thieving old hag, I'll get you, see if I don't!

Exits, at a run.

Meggie What was it that you were saying about a bear?

Mrs Briggs I thought I heard one earlier, unless I'm goin' mad.

Edmund Speaking as a doctor, I can assure you that you are perfectly sane. Master Valentine and I have actually seen the bear with our own eyes. It came rushing from the bushes.

Meggie Oh, no!

Mrs Briggs Shush. Listen again and we might hear it.

They all listen. Nothing.

Aubrey Oh, for pity's sake. Timothy! What's happening?

Timothy (*offstage*) Hang on, I'm putting the rug on...

Aubrey Don't! Just growl, will you?

Meggie I'm frightened! I don't want to see a bear.

Aubrey Fear not, fair maiden, I will protect you.

Meggie How? You haven't even got a sword.

Timothy (*offstage*) Right, I've done it. Grrrrrrrrr!

Mrs Briggs Help! Run!

All Aaargh! The bear, the bear!

All exit, pursued again by **Timothy** *in a furry rug.*

Act Four

Morning. Twittering birds. A country road, with a tree. There is a milestone engraved LONDON – 3. Enter **Dot** *with the basket, the barrel, the doctor's bag and her hook on a pole. She is still wearing Aubrey's hat.*

Dot Mornin' at last! Phew! What a night I've 'ad. Traipsing through the dark forest, stuffin' pie an' swiggin' mead, draggin' me poor old bones along. Took me hours to shake 'em off. Still, at least I didn't meet a bear.

She sits on the milestone.

I've scoffed all the food. The eggs fried up lovely. Shame all the mead's gone.

Now all I got is two empty baskets, an empty barrel, the doctor's bag and a fancy hat. I'll flog 'em down the market. Should get a decent price for the medical bag. All them knives and hacksaws; the murderers'll be queuin' up. I might 'ang on to the hat. I think it suits me... oh, my lawks! Who's this comin'? Best hide me stash.

She hides her ill-gotten goods behind a tree. She snatches off Aubrey's hat and throws it behind the tree as **Timothy** *enters as a pompous* **Justice of the Peace**. *He wears a robe and a wig.*

Timothy Good morrow, old mother. A fine morning.

Dot And who might you be, in yer fancy clobber?

Timothy My name is Sir Roger Fitzpodgerly and I represent the law in these parts, so mind your manners.

Dot Oooh! Right. Sorry, yer lordship. Didn't know you was a bigwig.

Timothy Well, I am. You may grovel now.

Dot Oh, I will, I will. (*Bobs a curtsy.*) Good day, yer honour, good day. Lovely robes, yer excellency. What are you, a judge or somethin'?

Timothy I happen to be a Justice of the Peace.

Dot Piece o' what?

Timothy Peace, mistress, peace. The short thing that comes between wars.

Dot Oh, that. Don't see a lot of it these days, do we, yer highness?

Timothy Indeed we do not. These are troubled times.

Dot Oh, they are, they are.

Timothy Crime is rife. Theft in

particular is up.

Dot Oh, it is, it is. Shockin' state of affairs. Can't trust no one.

Timothy At the last Quarter Session, I heard one hundred cases. Sixty per cent were for theft, ten per cent for burglary, three per cent for highway robbery, five per cent for murder and five per cent for witchcraft.

Dot I don't think that adds up right.

Timothy Quite. Nothing about crime adds up, as we men of law know only too well.

Dot Sounds like an important job, yer worship.

Timothy Oh, it is. We have to see to the dull things, too, y'know; making sure the roads are repaired and hedges put up. But mostly it's all about bringing thieves to justice.

Dot You're good at spottin' 'em,
I expect? Them wicked thieves?

Timothy Oh yes. I have an eagle eye.
Trained, you see. There's not much
passes me by.

Dot Ooh, I'll bet. Do you bring poor,
homeless old women to justice, too?

Timothy Most certainly. Us JPs deal
harshly with vagabonds and thieves of
either sex. In fact, we're probably tougher
on women, if anything. By the way,
forgive my curiosity, but what is the
purpose of that hook on a pole?

Dot Fendin' off bears. Terrible trouble
we 'ave with 'em 'ereabouts. And where
are you off to now, if you don't mind
my asking?

Timothy I go to London Town for
another Quarter Session, where a whole
bunch of light-fingered criminals await
judgement. Heads will roll, old mother,

heads will roll.

Dot I'll bet. Them naughty rogues'll be shiverin' in their shoes...

She breaks off at an outraged offstage shout.

Aubrey That's her! There she is, look!

Enter **Aubrey, Edmund, Mrs Briggs** *and* **Meggie. Dot** *gives a frightened squeal.*

Dot Oo-er! That's torn it.

Mrs Briggs You stole my pie, you old rascal!

Edmund My medical bag! Where is it?

Meggie What have you done with my eggs?

Aubrey Where's my hat?

Timothy Would somebody care to explain what is going on here?

Edmund And who might you be, sir?

Timothy Sir Roger Fitzpodgerly, sir. I am a Justice of the Peace.

Edmund Excellent! Well met, sir. We have need of your services. My name is Doctor Edmund Leech. I wish to report a heinous crime.

Aubrey I think you'll find that's my line.

Edmund Too late, I've said it.

Dot *gives a wail and falls to her knees.*

Dot Oh, no! Don't shop me! I didn't mean it, I wasn't thinkin', it's just a habit, I'll get help, I promise! Have pity on a poor old woman, always on the road…

Mrs Briggs I think you trotted out that sob story before. Round about the time you was scoffing my pie!

Aubrey And interfering with my hat!

Edmund And setting my leeches loose!

Meggie You shouldn't have taken our stuff, Dot. It was a horrible thing to do.

Dot I know that now! I've learned me lesson! Don't turn me in! (*She weeps.*)

Timothy Are you accusing that woman of stealing your property, sir? Because we take a grim view of that sort of thing around here.

Aubrey One moment, sir. We need to consult.

They go into a huddle and whisper. Finally, they reach a decision and break apart.

Timothy Well?

Edmund Your services will not be…

Aubrey (*firmly*) Excuse me. My line, I think. Your services will not be required, Sir Roger. Nobody will be arrested here today.

Dot Oh, thank you, thank you!

Timothy But I thought you said she had taken property belonging to you?

Aubrey Ah. Well, we did. But the fact is, sir, we are rehearsing a play.

Timothy A play?

Aubrey That's right. We're just a bunch of strolling actors. We practise as we stroll along. You stumbled upon us and mistook our theatrics for real life.

Timothy You are actors?

Aubrey We are. Some better than others, of course.

Timothy (*chuckling*) A play, eh? Well, well. You certainly had me convinced.

Aubrey Ah, but that's an actor's job. To be convincing.

Timothy Talking of jobs, I must away. Now all that's sorted out. I have villains to hang, witches to dunk, thieves to shout at.

Dot That's right, sir. You go off an' give them nasty thieves a good tickin' off!

Timothy I will. Good day to you all. A play, eh? Well, well.

He exits, still chuckling.

Dot (*shouting*) Don't forget to take yer eagle eye!

Everyone turns on **Dot**.

Edmund I don't know why you're sounding so cocky. As a doctor, I prescribe a strong dose of humility.

Aubrey Where have you hidden all our stuff?

Dot (*crestfallen*) Behind the tree.

Crossly, they recover their possessions.

Meggie All my eggs are gone. Oh, Dot, how could you?

Aubrey Look at my hat! You've bent all the feathers! It really is too bad. I've a good mind to run after Sir Roger and tell him the truth.

Dot Oh, no! No!

Mrs Briggs We got you off the hook. You could say sorry.

Dot I am, I am. I won't do it again, I promise. Thanks for not grassin' me up.

Sorry I took yer hat, Mr Valentine.

Aubrey Oh well. I suppose I forgive you. The quality of mercy is not strained. Actually, I pinched that line from Shakespeare. I'll have to come up with something similar.

Dot Um – all right if I keep the empty barrel?

Aubrey I suppose so.

Dot *collects the barrel.*

Edmund You're fortunate the landlord isn't here, old woman. I don't think he would have been so forgiving.

Dot Where is he, anyway?

Meggie We lost him in the forest. Probably eaten by the bear.

Edmund Enough talk. As a doctor, I recommend we leave this dreary spot and continue on our way. London awaits!

And a long queue of people waiting to be bled. (*Examines his bag of leeches.*) My babies are eager to be fed.

They all make to walk offstage. **Meggie** *hangs behind.*

Mrs Briggs Come on, Meggie love.

Meggie Not much point in me carrying on, now I haven't got eggs to sell.

Mrs Briggs Oh, don't be like that. At least you can go home saying you've seen the River Thames.

Edmund And the slums and the open sewers.

Mrs Briggs You might even catch a glimpse of Her Majesty. You'd like that, wouldn't you? Think of the tale you'll 'ave to tell, back on the farm. Ain't that right, Master Valentine?

Aubrey Quite right, Mrs Briggs. We've

come this far together, it would be folly to give up now, Meggie.

Mrs Briggs Come on, love. It ain't far. Only three more miles.

Meggie All right. I suppose so.

Aubrey That's the spirit! Come on, everyone. Let's go to London!

All exit.

Act Five

London. A bridge over the River Thames.
Enter **Aubrey**, **Edmund**, **Mrs Briggs**,
Meggie *and* **Dot**. *Bells are ringing in the*
distance.

Aubrey At last. London! London,
London, London! Do you hear the bells?

Mrs Briggs I can smell the smells, too.
Lawks, that river stinks, don't it?

Edmund Personally, I shall be glad to
get back to civilisation. If you look down
river at the far bank, you can see my
club, where I shall shortly be enjoying a
well-earned drink before performing a
series of terrifying operations on the

general public.

Mrs Briggs And I'll take up my housekeeper's position. On a chair with me feet up, hopefully.

Meggie And I suppose I'll go back to the farm.

Dot Dunno what I'll do. Now I'm a changed character and can't go round nickin' stuff. Probably starve.

Aubrey And I shall rejoin the Lord Chamberlain's Men. Ah, how sad it will be to part from such good friends. But there you go. All good things must come to an end.

He steps forward and addresses the audience.

> Alas, my friends! The time has come
> For us to end our play.
> The sun has set. 'Tis time for us
> To wend our weary w—

Meggie What are you doing?

Aubrey I'm winding the play up. Why?

Mrs Briggs That's it? It's ended?

Aubrey Well – yes. We've got to London.

Mrs Briggs And we all go home?

Aubrey Well – yes.

Mrs Briggs That's rubbish, that is.

Aubrey I beg your pardon?

Mrs Briggs We've come all this way and nothing interestin' happens? What kind of an ending is that?

Edmund I couldn't agree more. As a doctor, I prescribe a satisfying conclusion to our journey.

Meggie Yes. Something dramatic.

Aubrey That's all very well to say. Endings are hard. I'd like to see you come up with something.

Mrs Briggs I bet we could, too.

Edmund Certainly we could. For example, one of you could drown in the Thames. Not me, I'm the doctor, I'll be needed to write out the death certificate.

Mrs Briggs Too morbid. What about if Meggie falls in love with Master Valentine?

Meggie No, thanks.

Dot (*hopefully*) I could nick something else.

All NO!

Mrs Briggs 'Ere! I've got it! What if Timothy comes on as Queen Elizabeth. A surprise royal visit. Can't get more dramatic than meetin' the queen.

Aubrey Out of the question. These are Tudor times. It is forbidden to represent the reigning monarch on stage.

Mrs Briggs Even if she stays out of sight and shouts from the side?

Aubrey Absolutely not.

Meggie Even if she's in disguise?

Aubrey No, no, no! I'll just say the couplets and we'll end it here. Then I'll show it to Master Shakespeare. I'm hoping he'll agree to put it on. Mind you, there are one or two small wrinkles I need to iron out first.

Mrs Briggs You can say that again. That business with the landlord and the bear needs sorting. And Dot gets to say too much.

Dot Not now. I've gone all humble.

Edmund I still feel it needs something more. A surprise twist.

Meggie Maybe the bear could come on again and chase us all off.

Aubrey No. No more bear.

Mrs Briggs I still think it should be

Queen Elizabeth.

Aubrey I said, no! I'll get into trouble. Oh, good grief. What did I just say? Get off, Timothy.

A mysterious figure in a hooded cloak enters. Underneath the cloak, it is wearing a dress. This is **Timothy** *as* **Good Queen Bess** *in disguise.*

Timothy Too late. I've got the dress on now.

Aubrey I said, get off!

Timothy No. I want to be Good Queen Bess.

Aubrey You can't. It's not allowed. Anyway, I haven't written her any lines.

Timothy That's all right, I'll make them up.

Aubrey You will not. Kindly stop tampering with my play. It's not your head that'll be on the block. Get off.

Timothy No. I want a decent scene. I've hardly had any good lines.

Aubrey But you said you didn't want to play females.

Timothy I've changed my mind. (*He speaks in imperious, falsetto tones.*) Her Majesty gets very annoyed when crossed, so have a care if you value your head.

Aubrey Stop it, will you.

Edmund Oh, let him be the queen if he wants.

Timothy Queen? We didn't say we were the queen. No, we are just a lady. A very ordinary, mysterious passing lady who is definitely not the queen in disguise. We decided to de-barge and take a little stroll on the riverbank. We had no inkling that we would come across a bunch of commoners. We're quite excited. Who are you all, pray?

Aubrey That's it. I've finally lost control.

Edmund (*dropping to his knees and kissing* **Timothy***'s hand*) Dr Edmund Leech. Your servant, madam.

Timothy (*wiping his hand on his dress*) Well, yes, obviously. Everyone is, we know that. And the rest of you?

Edmund Allow me to make the introductions…

Aubrey Oh no, you don't. If we're having the queen, *I'm* doing the talking. Ma'am, allow me to introduce myself and my companions. I am Aubrey Valentine, professional actor. This is Mrs Briggs, Meggie Wilkins and Dot Doxy.

Timothy Enchanted. Have you come far?

Aubrey We have indeed, madam.

Timothy And do you like London?

Mrs Briggs Well, we've only just arrived. We had a bad time getting here. Public transport's nonexistent. The roads are shockin'. The taverns are filthy. And there's bears in the woods.

Timothy Oh, really? How inconvenient. We really must do something about that.

Aubrey Surely you mean – *the queen* must do something about it.

Timothy Yes. That's what we meant, although we don't much like being corrected. So, you have experienced many inconvenient perils on your journey, you say?

Aubrey Indeed we have. Would you like to hear about them?

Timothy No, we don't think so, but thank you for drawing them to our attention. It is important to occasionally listen to the whinings of the common people if we are to avoid revolution. Leave it with us, we will think on it. And now we must move on. We have a lot of pressures on our time. And quite a lot of pressure on our waist, too. These Tudor gowns are very uncomfortable. So nice to meet you. Goodbye – goodbye…

Exit **Good Queen Bess**, *waving in queenly fashion. The cast wave until she is out of sight. Everyone is in shock.*

Meggie That was her, wasn't it? Her in disguise.

Mrs Briggs You mean – that was – nah! Surely not!

Dot I think it was, y'know.

Edmund Speaking as a doctor, there is no doubt in my mind that we have been in the presence of our glorious monarch. Oh, happy, happy day!

Dot *peers offstage.*

Dot She's getting into 'er barge, look. She's taken 'er cloak off, I can see 'er ginger wig!

Mrs Briggs There she goes. See the

crowds gathering on the opposite bank?
You can hear 'em cheering!

Aubrey We should add our merry voices
to the general clamour, don't you think?
Huzza! God save the queen! God save
the queen!

All God save the queen! God save the
queen!

*They wave and shout at the barge until it
rounds the bend.*

Meggie I can't believe it! I met Good
Queen Bess!

Mrs Briggs You see? I bet you're glad
you came to London now.

Dot Seemed all right, didn't she? Down
to Earth. I bet she don't sort out the
transport, though.

Aubrey Well, we've met the queen,
although I'm still not convinced we
should have, and I really think that

provides a fitting climax to the play. All right, Timothy, you can come on again. We're winding up. I'm about to do the final couplets.

Enter **Timothy**, *carrying his cloak.*

Dot And then we get paid, right?

Edmund Yes, I was wondering about that.

Aubrey Later. When we're in the tiring room.

Edmund I'm afraid I must insist upon payment now. I am a busy man and I can't wait for the couplets. I have enjoyed performing in your play, Master Valentine – an interesting diversion, but my part is done. My money, if you please.

Sighing, **Aubrey** *pulls out a purse and pays* **Edmund**. *The rest hold their hands out. He pays them, too.*

Aubrey There. Satisfied?

Edmund Thank you. I leave you with these words. Wrap up warm and keep taking the medicine.

Meggie What medicine? You haven't given us any medicine.

Edmund It's just something we doctors say. (*Goes to leave. Stops.*) Oh! My card, Master Valentine. If ever you feel unwell, look me up and I'll experiment on you. I can't say fairer than that.

He gives a business card to **Aubrey**.

Mrs Briggs What about us? Don't we get a card?

Edmund No. You can't read.

Meggie We wouldn't mind one for a souvenir, though.

Edmund Not a chance. These are Tudor times. Paper's expensive.

Mrs Briggs Where are you going, Dot? When the play's over?

Dot I'm off to flog the empty barrel down the market. I'll cunningly fill it with Thames water first, o' course. Ain't no flies on me.

Edmund There are, you know.

Meggie I thought you were a changed character.

Dot Nah. Not really. That only 'appens in plays.

They all go to leave.

Aubrey Hold it! Nobody goes anywhere until I say the final lines. And then we take our bows.

Edmund We take a bow? Oh, well that's different. I'll hang on for that.

Aubrey All right, Timothy, come on again now. I'm about do the couplets.

*Enter **Timothy**, carrying his cloak.*
Everyone stands in line. **Aubrey** *steps*
forward and addresses the audience.

Alas, my friends! The time has come
    For us to end our play.
    The sun has set. 'Tis time for us
    To wend our weary way.

Our tale is done. The curtain falls
To loud and ringing cheers.

Meggie We spent a lot o' time with you.

Timothy Sometimes it felt like years.

Edmund The time has come for us to part.
We hope you liked our play.

Aubrey So raise your voices one last time.
Hip, hip, hip…

All Hooray!

The cast take their curtain call, to loud and sustained rejoicing.

Epilogue

The cast relax in the tiring room.

Mrs Briggs Do you think they liked it?

Edmund Who knows?

Dot *I* think they liked it.

Meggie Well, they ought to. We did our best, didn't we?

Mrs Briggs I quite enjoyed it. Made a change from cooking. Well done, Master Valentine.

Aubrey It needs a little more work, I think. Before I show it to Shakespeare.

Timothy I thought it was all right,

actually. A bit confusing here and there.

Aubrey Only because you wouldn't stick to the script.

Timothy But I reckon it was all right. A couple of tweaks, and you just might have a hit on your hands. Can I take this dress off now?

The End

About the Author

Kaye Umansky has written over 100 books for children, including picture books, poetry, novels, music books and plays. Probably best known for the very funny *Pongwiffy* books, she has contributed four plays to the *Curtain Up!* series (A & C Black) and has written a number of music books, including *Three Tapping Teddies*, *Three Singing Pigs* and *Three Rapping Rats*, winner of the TES Schoolbook Award for Primary Music. Her novel *The Silver Spoon of Solomon Snow* won the 2005 Spoken Word Award. Kaye taught in primary schools for many years, specialising in music and drama. She has written full-time for the last 20 years and lives in London with her husband Mo, her daughter Ella and two cats, Alfie and Heathcliff.

Year 5

The Path of Finn McCool • Sally Prue

The Barber's Clever Wife • Narinder Dhami

Taliesin • Maggie Pearson

Fool's Gold • David Calcutt

Time Switch • Steve Barlow and Steve Skidmore

Let's Go to London! • Kaye Umansky

Year 6

Shock Forest and Other Stories • Margaret Mahy

Sky Ship and Other Stories • Geraldine McCaughrean

Snow Horse and Other Stories • Joan Aiken

Macbeth • Tony Bradman

Romeo and Juliet • Michael Cox

The Tempest • Franzeska G. Ewart